MW00946923

Breaking the Cycles of Abandonment:
I am NOT My Father

The story of a man's journey into fatherhood

Melvin L. White

Published by Legacy Builders Speakers

Cover Design and Photography by Garret Kisner Studios

Breaking the Cycles of Abandonment: I am NOT My Father, The story of a man's journey into fatherhood

Copyright ©2014 by Melvin L. White

Published by Legacy Builders Speakers, 3262 East 132nd, Cleveland, OH 44120

Cover design and photography by Garret Kisner Studios, Cleveland, OH
Printed by CreateSpace Independent Publishing Platform

ISBN-13: 978-1495340482
ISBN-10: 1495340481

All rights reserved. No part of this publication may be reproduced, stored in a retrieval system, or transmitted, in any form or by any means, electronic, mechanical, photocopying, recording or otherwise, without the prior permission of the publishers.

Printed in the United States

To my Husband:

I wanted to congratulate you on fulfilling a dream of becoming an author. You are truly one of the bravest and most caring men I have ever met. Opening up your heart to some of the deepest and painful moments in your life really took a strong belief in God and a commitment to helping others.

Reading this book made me reflect back on how important you have been in my life and even more importantly in the lives of our daughters. You have instilled in their spirit how to walk with purpose because of your commitment to being their father. The foundation that you have laid as a father will always be embedded in their core and it is that foundation that carries them throughout their life's journey.

We have often talked about growing up without our fathers and it makes me so proud to witness your relationship with the girls. It has always been a dream to have a relationship with my dad like you have with our girls. I truly believe that each one of our girls are secure in who they are because of your presence in their lives.

We have transition our blended family into one core structure and I truly believe this happened because of your unwavering desire to ensure there would never be a feeling of the word STEP in our house. These are our children and you are their FATHER and they have never doubted your love or your commitment to each and every one of them.

When I look at you and the work that you do for our children and others it makes me so proud because I know that I am looking at a man. You are a man that takes responsibility for his actions regardless of the consequences. You are a man that stands for what he believes no matter the cost. You are a man that your daughters are proud to call DAD and that I am proud to call my husband.

Thank you for giving me almost two decades of support, strength, and the desire to be the best mom, wife and friend. I love you and I am so proud to be your wife and the mother to our children.

-Nicole

Contents

108

Reader's Guide for Breaking the Cycle of
Abandonment
Discussion Questions
110

Foreword

For the past two decades, I have been teaching at a diverse group of colleges and universities here in Cleveland, Ohio. I have worked, for example, with students at Case Western Reserve University, a well-funded, private institution with students who are well-prepared for the college experience. I have also taught students at Cuyahoga Community College, an urban school generally serving the less privileged. With many of these students, and across all of their various differences, I have experienced first-hand the often negative effects of dominant, American ideas about male gender identity. These are young men unsure of their economic futures, unsure of their relations to the women in their lives and typically feeling great pressure to ignore the many rich facets of their emotional lives. For those of these men raised in environments riddled with addiction, physical and mental violence and fathers and other male role models who are less-than-present in their lives, the effects are even more damaging. A widespread lack of emotional intelligence seems to plague many young men of all walks of life. It is within this environment that the appearance of this new book by Melvin White, *Breaking the Cycles of Abandonment: I am NOT My Father*, is so striking.

This is a powerful and unique text. Melvin humbly walks the reader through his boyhood pain of an absent father and a string of violent male role models, his attempts in later life to love a woman with an addiction and his battles to protect his young daughters and provide them with the love they need. These are gripping struggles to be loved, to give love and to provide love going forward into the future.

Breaking the Cycles of Abandonment has much to offer. Appearing through the prose, we meet a genuine, self-reflecting and honest man working through love and life. He vividly demonstrates that a man can indeed wrestle through a complex emotional life and come to terms with what it *can* mean to be a son, a man and a father. He gives clear and prescient advice to other fathers that may be facing similar challenges. The book might also serve as an effective teaching tool, a guide of sorts for young men facing the additional challenges of college life. What we learn as men from this book is that we don't have to be oblivious victims of our own emotional lives. We *can* come to understand our emotions (as we try to do with our intellectual lives) and marshal them to the service of a healthy and strong way of life.

-Paul W. Hanson, Ph.D.

Thanks and Acknowledgements

To my mom, Arlene, who had to sacrifice so much of her own life to make sure I had a chance in life. We really did grow up together Ma. I love you so much.

To my stepfather Norman who came into my life when I was eighteen and showed me what a real man should be. I love you and thank you.

To my children, Desiree, Yssis and Taylor, thank you all for helping me become the best Dad I could be. I know I made some mistakes along the way, but we hung in there together. I love you all with all my heart.

To my wife, Nicole, thank you for being my rock and a calming voice when I get out of control. Thank you for not giving up on me even when I was giving up on myself. I love you and God knew I needed you.

To my father, thank you for helping me to see that I could break the cycle and become a father to my daughters.

To my brother Mike, we have had our struggles, but I am so proud of the father you have become. Love you MAN!

Introduction

The feeling of being abandoned is not a race or a class issue; it's the reality of the world in which we live. Blacks, Whites, Hispanics, Native Americans, gays, straights, rich and poor- all face abandonment. The scariest part about growing up in a neighborhood like I did is that most people simply adapt. If you never had a strong fatherly presence, then how do you know what you are missing? In many ways, my story relates to the stories of people from all walks of life. Many of us might be connected by my story because of our experiences and desires to seek change. Read this book and understand that regardless of the circumstances, we can all make a choice to do something different in our lives.

1

Abandoned

One dictionary definition of the word "abandonment" is to leave completely and finally; forsake utterly; desert: to abandon a child; to abandon a sinking ship.

I was abandoned by my father before I was even born. Imagine a fifteen year old female, pregnant and feeling alone and scared. At a time in her life when she should have been going on her first date or experiencing her first kiss, she was preparing to have her first child. This scared young pregnant mother to be was my mother, Arlene.

On August 25, 1968, I was born a premature and sickly child. I was born into yet another stereotype in our community. I am sure the headlines would have read: "Another young black child born to another single teenage mother in the inner city". Absent was the father. Absent was the male role model. Absent was the architect of the family structure. Absent was a father's desire to accept his first born, his foot print in life, and the successor to his legacy.

Like so many children in the inner city, I came into the world already at a disadvantage. I was black, I was a male, and I was fatherless. I was born Melvin Lee White. Unfortunately that was my mother's last name. I never had the privilege of carrying my father's name. Yes, the birth certificate carried his name, but he never signed the document. He never came to claim his heir to the name Rutledge.

From the moment I opened my eyes, I was abandoned. Yes, I had my mom, but she too was abandoned. She was abandoned by my father, who went on to be the fifteen year old kid hanging out and enjoying life. She was abandoned by her mother and stepfather because of her strong desire to care for her own child and not give custody to her parents. During my delivery, my grandmother told the nurse that she was going home and to call after my mother gave birth. She did not even stay to help my mother through the most terrifying moment of her life. My mom's decision not to surrender me forced her to leave home at sixteen.

Armed with a diaper bag and heavy heart, my mother set out to face the challenges of the world. Finding shelter with an older sister, my mother had to do whatever it took to make sure her new born son was okay. Having to abandon school in exchange for motherhood was a choice she had to make. Allowing public assistance to play the role of father was another decision forced on my mother. Having limited education hindered opportunities for her employment. My mother found temporary work with local neighborhood centers. She was an aid and cleaner at the neighborhood childcare center. The center allowed her to bring me to work and that was a major help because she did not have any one to care for me while she worked.

My mother would tell me the stories of how she had to walk to work so that she could save the bus fare to feed me that day. Sometimes as she walked, she would see my father continuing on with his life, not worrying about how we were doing. Even though she was frustrated and angered, she did not bash him. She simply said he was doing what he wanted to do and we were doing what we had to do. Life dealt us both a bad hand, but we had each other. Thanks dad for the abandonment. This is a poem just for my father.

Abandoned I Felt

Today I was born and as I looked at the faces of all the doctors, nurses and my mother, yours wasn't there. *Abandoned I felt!*
Today I opened my eyes and lifted my head checking to see if you were there, but you weren't. *Abandoned I felt!*
Today I crawled for the first time, but you didn't see me. *Abandoned I felt!*
Today I took my first steps and I looked to see if you were behind me, but you weren't. *Abandoned I felt!*
Today I said the words "dada", hoping you would come, but you never did. *Abandoned I felt!*
Today I heard my mommy cry and I prayed that you would come and wipe the tears from her eyes, but you never came. *ABANDONED WE FELT!*

To all fathers: do you want this poem to be how your child thinks of you? Think about it long and hard!!!

2

A Father for Me Too

My mom and I faced the world's challenges as a team. As I began to grow, I had numerous medical conditions. I had seizures and I spent many days in the hospital. The doctors often told my mom that I would always be underweight and sickly.

During her time caring for me, my mom met a young man and began dating. She and Mike dated for a year and at the age of nineteen; my mother gave birth to my brother Michael. Our world would forever change. She married my brother's dad and now I had a father too. I remember him buying things for us and I was happy to have a father. Mike would take me for a ride in his big car and man was I feeling good! My new dad was this great big man, not like the skinny little guy that was my biological dad. I had a big strong dad and he wanted to be with us. This was the best feeling a four year old could ever imagine.

But the feeling did not last long. Mike became verbally and physically abusive. He would beat my mom and all I could do was cry. Imagine a five year old boy holding his baby brother and crying and wishing that he never prayed for a father. After the beating, he would act as if nothing happened. He would tell my mom how much he loved her and that she was the one who made him act like that.

At one point, Mike convinced my mom that everything would be okay if we just left Ohio. We moved to Alexander City, Alabama. I was almost finished with second grade when we moved. I remember telling my grandma how scared I was to leave. My mom was so happy because she really wanted this marriage to work. We stayed with Mike's family, and for a while I thought we would be okay.

Before I could start school in the fall, the abuse was unleashed again, and the fear and panic returned again. Mike drank and drank and that was never a good sign for my mom. His family tried to shield my brother and me from the rage of Mike, but I knew that face. I had seen this mad man before. I knew that I wanted to get my mom and brother out of this hell. One day my grandma called to talk to me and I remember whispering trying to tell her how mean Mike was to mommy. I told her I wanted to come back home. I told her I was scared and she needed to help mommy. The verbal abuse occurred more often than the physical. I now know that verbal and mental abuse can cause just as much damage as physical abuse.

My grandmother talked to my mom about leaving, and with the help of Mike's sister we were able to escape and return to Cleveland. Once again we moved in with my aunt and attempted to put the fear behind us. My mom attempted to piece her life back together. Now it was the three of us and the pressure to be a good mother was even greater. My grandmother would help a little, but it was not like a real family unit.

Part of my mom getting her life back together meant getting out into the social scene. My mom had no problems finding men that were attracted. Even though she dated, my mom always made sure that my brother and I had the things we needed. I remember when holidays would come and my grandma would invite us over; my mother's pride would not allow us to go. She would tell us "When you see your grandma and she asks what you all ate for the holidays, you better say you ate ribs, mac and cheese and greens. When in reality we had neck bones and rice. Sometimes when things were really tight she would let us go visit my grandma to eat; she would stay home alone in hunger. Pride is something else!

3

God, are You Hearing My Prayers?

Finally, my mother decided to end things with Mike. She was granted a divorce and now was free to move forward. Someone forgot to tell Mike that they were no longer married. He returned from Alabama and began harassing my mom, telling her that she would always be his wife.

I remember asking God to please just make him go away and to find us someone who would love and protect our family. Then Thomas appeared on the scene, my hero. Thomas was a man that took care of my mom and he was not afraid of Mike. I thought that God had sent Thomas to protect us from Mike. Thomas took us to church and bought us nice clothes; he seemed to be a good man. I was so happy that Thomas was coming to protect us. My new dad! Yeah right!!!

It was not long before Thomas wanted to be a father to my mom instead of a man. He began to dictate what she wore and who she could have as friends. He started with verbal abuse and soon it became physical. "Why, God would you place so much pain upon our family", I asked? I remember when my mom tried to leave Thomas. He told her he would kill her before he would let her leave. We were living in an apartment building and Thomas was parked outside our house with his gun. My mom told me to take my brother and go to the back of the house and no matter what happens do not come out. My mom boiled a pot of scolding hot water and she just waited for him to break down our door. Thank you God for not letting anything happen on that night.

My mom went back and forth with Thomas before they finally left each other alone. There were a few more Thomas' along the way; maybe not the same name but the same outcome. Mr. Jessie, Mr. Henry, Mr. White, Mr. Larry, and Mr.

Roy were some of the men in my mom's life. They did not live with us but they all had an impact. The amazing part of this story is that none of these men ever spent any time with my brother and me. Mr. White was a good guy; he really cared about my mom. Yet, of course, he was the one she misused. I did not understand how she could take all that crap from the men that did not care for her and then turn around and abuse the one that did!

Mr. Roy was the man that my mom seemed to like the most, and he moved in with our family. I never liked him and I trusted him even less. I would see him out with other women and he did not care. He was a drunk and a cheat, but hell my mom was doing the same thing. He and my mom lived together for years. When I was in the 6th grade, Mr. Roy came home drunk and started an argument. He started to come towards her as if he was going to hit her. I knew that there would never come a time again that I would be helpless in defending my mother. I took my stick and I started beating the hell out of Mr. Roy. I remember thinking how much I wanted to beat him for all the times I could not beat Mike and Thomas. After the fight, Mr. Roy moved out.

A few weeks passed, and, as always, she forgave him and he moved back into the house. She would always say, "Baby sometimes we do what we have to do not what we want to do. When you get older you will understand." I finally did understand those words.

I often wondered why these men did not want to be a part of our lives. We were not bad kids. Why did they only want my mom and not us? God is this how all men treat kids? I often prayed that if I ever had children I would be a good father and love them with all my heart.

Coming into my teenage years were rough because I never experienced going to a basketball or football game with my father. I never experienced learning how to drive at sixteen. I never experienced the sex talk!! I just experienced a neighborhood with young black males that looked like me and mothers that looked like my mother. The fathers simply did not exist. The male role models did not come and show us how to respect our mothers; they did not come and show us how to catch a ball; they did not come and tell us about becoming a man. Often what was learned came from the streets and older fatherless peers and that was not always good. They showed us how to fight, how to sell drugs, and how to be a menace to society.

God, why did I hear the painful sounds of my friend's mothers screaming at them, "You're just like your father. You ain't shit and you ain't gonna be shit". I often heard them being victimized for looking like their fathers or sounding like their fathers or acting like their fathers. I looked like my father, but my mom did not hold it against me. She never really talked about my father too much. She would always say that he was doing what he wanted to do in life.

4

God had a Plan for Me

My mother challenged me my whole life to be the best student and the best person that I could be. She did not let her not finishing high school become an excuse for me to mess-up. I did not always accept the challenge, and I sometimes faltered, but by the grace of God I never failed too badly. I understood that I never wanted to disappoint the woman that sacrificed so much. I remember the first time I did disappoint my mother. I was in the eighth grade and my mother had given me money to go downtown to Woolworth's to get some items for her. I decided that I was going to steal the items and keep the money. I had seen my cousin steal, so it could not be that difficult. I stole all the items on my mom's list and then I went to May Company to test my skills again. I stole a bracelet for my girlfriend and got away with it. I really got bold and went back to steal the matching necklace. I started walking to the door and plain clothes officers asked me to come with them. They took me to a room and handcuffed me to a bench.

I remember the female security person searching me and finding all the items that I had stolen during my spree. I began to lie and tell them that my bag had been torn so all the items had to go into my pockets. They finally found the jewelry that I had stolen from them.

During that search, the lady also found my report card and saw that I was an Honor Roll student. She began to slap me upside my head repeating, "Why would you disgrace your mother and father who have worked so hard to raise you and keep you from being like these bad ass kids out here". She just assumed that I had a father in the home because I was a good student. That was the first time I truly began to think in a certain way about what it would be like to have a father. Could he have taught me to respect my environment? Could I blame what's happening on the fact that I did not have a dad?

The officer asked for my information to call my parents and I told her that it was only my mom and she looked so shocked. I asked her if there was any way we could not call my mom. She said no! This was the first time I had to face my mom in shame. My mom had to have my aunt bring her to May Company because she did not drive. I think that was the biggest embarrassment for my mom because now the family was going to become aware of my actions. When they arrived my aunt got to preaching about how ashamed and disappointed she was in me. My mom never said a word to me. She spoke to the security lady and made a deal with her for me to come and clean the security office after school. The store didn't press charges, because I was a good student and had never been in trouble. All the way home, I remember hearing my aunt fussing and my mom being silent.

When my aunt dropped us off, my mom thanked her and we went into the house. She told me to go to my room and take off my clothes. I went in the room and I took off my pants and shirt. My mom came in and said takeoff everything. I remember whispering, "I'm too old to be getting a whoopin". She said, "Boy you will take it off or I will shoot you where you stand". I cried and said, "I'm a man now mama and you shouldn't do this". She said a man would never steal, lie, and humiliate his family. My mom tore my butt up and the pain I saw in her face hurt me worse than the pain from the beating. For the first time I realized that I had no idea of what it meant to be a man. I did not have a father to guide me through this stage of my life. At that point, I promised myself that I would never hurt my mother like that again.

I began to understand that we all have the chance to make the right or wrong decisions. And, we know when we have made either one of them. I told myself that whatever I do in life I will own the decisions I make. I will never use not having a father or growing up in poverty as an excuse for bad decisions. I understood that my mom could have made excuses to me for having to be a single parent. Yet, she did not. She took pride in raising me and I had to take pride in being her son.

Life took some ups and downs for me, but since that time, I have tried never to make excuses for my decisions. The thought of having a father now crept into my mind regularly. I wanted a father to teach me how to tie a tie. I wanted him to take me for a ride and sneak and let me get behind the wheel. I wanted him to tell me "Boy, listen to your mother". Those conversations never came. The men in my mom's life never took on those responsibilities, but mom always had my back.

I remember when she got her monthly welfare check. She would walk my brother and me to the department store and we would put clothes in layaway and we would stop for burgers and fries. Those were some good days. I hold those memories close to my heart.

My junior year of high school created new challenges for me to keep my promise not to hurt my mother again. Crack had come into our community, and man it was a big deal. Most of my friends began selling the drug and were making a lot of money. I started to see what they were buying for their moms and I was envious of the material things. My one friend Steve had brought a car and a truck. He had them totally tricked out; man, he was the shit in the neighborhood. He was getting all the girls and all the guys respected him.

I saw a change in the mothers in the neighborhood too. They began to dress better and they began to reap the rewards from their sons' drug deals. I wondered if my mother would let me sell drugs to help out the family. I talked to my mom about all the stuff that everyone was getting and I asked her if she wanted to have the jewelry and the clothes that all the other moms were wearing. My mother looked at me and said, "Boy, all I need is for you to stay focused and go to school." I told her that I could do both and she told me that she did not want me to think that little of myself and of the people that crack affected.

I listened to my mom's advice and did not try to sell crack. I landed a job at a record store and I was able to buy clothes for my brother and me. I was able to help my mom with some of the bills. I made sure that my brother Mike had everything he needed. I was his big brother and it was my responsibility to take care of him. I still hung out with my friends even though they sold drugs. The pressure to be like them was strong. I wanted to sell drugs and get a fly ride. I had a decision to make: was I going to keep making minimum wage and never get a ride like Steve's, or was I going to hurt my mother? Needless to say, I never got the fly ride. But somewhere in the pit of my stomach I never stopped believing that God had a plan for me. I am glad I did not sell crack.

I saw what crack was doing to my community and I did not want to be a part of that group. Unfortunately, crack had taken hold of a lot of my family members and the results were devastating. Aunts, cousins and uncles fell one by one to that powerful hit. Crack was like a plague and the entire community was infected. I had never seen such a powerful influence on so many people.

The biggest causality of crack was my MOM! My mom slowly became addicted to the powerful drug CRACK. I found myself starting to see her changing how she acted. She would claim monies had been stolen or lost. Even during her addiction my mother never stopped pushing me to be the best.

I would be so angry with her and the worst part of her addiction was she never saw herself as being a crack head. My mom battled with the use of crack and she finally kicked her habit. God thank you for giving me back my mom. Even through the pain and confusion; I knew God had a plan for me.

I would always pray, "God please tell me what your plan is for me". I felt so overwhelmed with trying not to be a part of the in crowd. During my struggles to battle the urge not to be a follower and wait for God's plans, my brother was headed for disaster.

5

Failing to Protect

Making the decision not to sell crack was a lot easier than facing the disappointment with myself for failing to protect my little brother from becoming a drug dealer. All the friends that used to hang with me started hanging with my brother. I did not like what I was seeing in Mike. He started getting in trouble and I knew he was on the block selling drugs. I talked to my mom and she was in denial. Mike and I started drifting apart and the communication seemed to be lost. He was no longer impressed with me talking about school and getting good grades. He was now listening to the dope boys, and their influence was powerful.

I started to notice a change in my mom. She was not that strong voice on my brother as she had been with me. She seemed to always justify the items he had or the items that I started seeing coming in the house. I went to her to let her know that he was cutting school and hanging with the wrong crowd. She just said, "baby, momma tired." I looked at her and wondered how could she be too tired to see what is happening. She was only 32 but she had gone through so much in those years.

I remembered screaming in my room "GOD WHAT DID I DO TO NOT HAVE A FATHER FOR MIKE AND ME?" If I had a father he would deal with Mike. I made up my mind that I was going to be his father and make him listen. The thought was great but it did not work. When I tried to tell Mike what to do it just caused us to fight. He was only 3 ½ years younger and he wanted me to realize I was not his father. The more I talked, the more he rebelled. Mike was truly on the road to self-destruction and I could only stand in fear.

The flow of drugs in the community really changed Mike's personality. He became so abrasive and controlling. What happened to my baby brother, who looked to me to protect him?

Mike was a force to be reckoned with. It appeared he had the respect from the streets and also the fear. My younger brother was driving nice cars and living the life while I was still riding the local bus. "God, what is going on in my life?" I asked again "What are your plans for me?"

Each day I watched my brother stand on the block selling drugs was another day I started to doubt whether or not a father would have made a difference. Even the men old enough to be our fathers were in some form of hustle. They too were victims of fatherless homes.

Mike served a year in jail unrelated to drugs. When he came home he was worse than ever. He was moving major weight and causing all kinds of disturbances for rival drug dealers. Once again my mother turned a blind eye and there was nothing I could do other than pray!

The life that Mike chose had a profound effect on the entire family. There were so many people looking to hurt my brother and I made every effort to be his protector. Eventually Mike's decisions hurt the entire family.

Mike's drug dealing hit home with my mom. Mike began to control the house. The argument my mom gave me when I thought about selling drugs escaped her when it came to Mike. She began accepting items from his drug transactions. The comfort level he had talking to my mom about drug deals and events was unbelievable. I started to feel like I was the outsider in our family. I eventually moved out of the house to avoid confrontational situations with Mike.

Eventually Mike's actions had an effect on me. When a person enters the drug life they develop many enemies. Some will camouflage themselves as friends. The one person that you might never suspect could be the person that does the most harm. Mike would often drink and get into altercations with his girlfriend. One day those altercations led to a physical confrontation with several of her friends. I attempted to help Mike deal with the altercation and it ended in me being shot. The amazing part of this drama was the fact that Mike's girlfriend was the person who shot me in the waist. And to think, I have a niece by this young lady, imagine our family reunions.

The second time Mike's altercation affected me was when rival dealers put a contract out on him. Mike had parked his car outside of my house and several rival drug dealers thought that he was in the house so they decided to seize the opportunity. My house was completely shot-up when rival drug dealers wanted to send Mike a message. The police counted over a 100 rounds of bullets that penetrated my walls. Amazingly no one was hit or, more importantly, killed.

The next day, in broad daylight, another attack took place on my house. Mike and several of my family members were there to help me clean up the damage and a rival dealer drove by and opened fire on the entire porch. Mike was shot in the face and I was shot in the back. This was the day that my mom almost lost both her sons.

After we both recovered, I moved from the neighborhood and Mike continued to sell drugs. I attempted to keep a close eye on Mike, but I understood that he must create his own path and I could not protect him. Sometimes all we can do is pray. God is still watching him.

The price that families pay for the sins of drug dealers is often more than the dealer pays. Mike's deals hit my mother's home hard. Mike and my mom lived in a two family home where Mike often hid his drugs. One day a young man knocked on the door inquiring about a classic car Mike had for sale. When my mother went to the door to get his information, she was forced back into the house at gunpoint. Once inside, two other men arrived and they tied my mom up along with Mike's girlfriend and child. These men knew exactly where Mike's drugs and money were hidden. They also knew not to tie my mother's legs too tight because she had bad ankles. One man told the other that her ankle is bad and to only tie her hands. The life of a drug dealer does not allow you to have real friends. This was clearly someone close to Mike and his operation. Again, I looked at my mom with confusion as to why she had allowed Mike to house drugs in her presence.

I again turned to God and said, "Please give me the strength to stand strong against my children if they are doing wrong. Please allow me to be a strong influence in their lives. Please give me the strength to not enable them. Please give me the courage to do whatever is needed to protect my own integrity and the standards of my household".

6

Breaking the Cycle of Abandonment

Breaking the cycle of abandonment is not an easy task. It requires commitment and dedication to being a father. The task becomes even more challenging when there are no positive role models to guide you. Yes, you can read hundreds of books on how to be a good father, but the fear within cannot be conquered by authors who have never faced these challenges. Trust me, I know what it is like to tremble and sweat thinking about all the ways you will mess-up this thing called fatherhood. The lack of trust that you had for the men that floated in and out of your life makes the pit of your stomach quiver. Scared that you never even learned what to say to a child other than the negative echoes that might have filled your home, your deepest fears are real. Believe me, I too had those fears.

The best way to help conquer those fears is to look in the mirror and believe that God is on your side. Ask him to guide you through and help you be the man you want to be for your child. Think about all the desires you had as a kid. Think about what you wanted from your father. Write down your thoughts and let that become your first map into fatherhood. It will need tweaking along the way, but it is a start. The biggest step is being there.

Trust me; children do not require a bunch of material items. They really just want your time and love. I can remember how many times I just wanted my father to simply be there for me. I would have given anything just to have him come to a game or sit and talk to me.

The greatest moment of my life was when I had the opportunity to break the cycle. I remember the relationship that brought my oldest daughter into the world as if it was yesterday. My journey into fatherhood started when I met my first wife Paula. I was a preschool teacher and Paula was there to enroll her daughter. She had on this brown skirt and some open toe sandals with legs for days. I remember turning to my friend and saying, "Man that is going to be my wife." Renee said, "You have a different girl every school year". I told her that this was different. It's something about her and I just felt a connection. Renee laughed and said, "Fool, she ain't even looking your way."

When she came over to the desk I introduced myself and she told me that her name was Paula and that her daughter was Shanequa. I watched her as she filled out the paperwork, thinking to myself what would be the best way to ask her to go out with me. I started talking to Shanequa and when it was time for her to leave; I made some silly comment to her mom. Paula just smiled but did not appear to be the least bit interested in me. My co-workers laughed and said, "Yeah, you really got her hot for you". I told them in time she would be my wife and that she would have my baby.

Every day she came to school was a day that I felt a little bit closer to her and Shanequa. We began having conversations about life and other situations. She told me that she had another daughter and a son. The thought of her having three kids did not change the feelings I was developing for her. Unfortunately, Paula did not show outwardly the same interest in me. Then one day I just asked for her number and she said, "No, but I will take yours."

A couple of weeks went by and she never called. I would make small conversation when I saw her to try and find out why. Then one day out of the blue she called. We talked and she told me that normally she would not have even talked to me because I was not her type. We joked on the phone and from that day forward we had a connection.

We had our first date and man was it a good one. She came over to my house and she was wearing a blue jeans skirt with black and brown riding boots and that body was all that! I was sprung and I was not mad. That night was one of the best nights we ever had together.

I went to work and told my co-workers, "I told y'all she was going to be my woman and it only took me a couple of months." I thought I was the man. I became a one woman man. My family was not happy with my decision to be involved in a readymade family, but it did not matter.

Paula lived at home with her mom and the three kids. None of the kids' dads were really in the picture. We started getting so close that I asked her to have my baby and she agreed. She was concerned about having another baby's daddy and living at home with her mom. I assured her that I would never abandon my responsibility as a father and that I would be a dad to the other kids.

The next month was Christmas and I remember going out and buying the kids all these Christmas gifts. I bought her a washer and dryer. I was happy to be in their lives. I really had a connection with her youngest child, Darius. He was the son I never had. We would hang out and I was doing all the things with him that my father never did with me. I was not going to be one of those guys I grew up watching come in and out of my life. I spent time with all the kids and Paula was so happy.

On New Year's Eve 1991, I went over to Paula's and when all the kids where sleep Paula took her shower and came downstairs with her lingerie on and man she was beautiful. I never will forget that night because that was the night I became A DAD! A FATHER! HAPPY NEW YEARS 1992!!!!

Life was great and I planned to spend it with Paula and the kids. Paula was pregnant and she had made me the happiest man in the world. I would try to work as many hours as I could because I wanted to get a place for me and my new family.

Some nights Paula could not sleep and we would go out and play basketball at 1or 2 am at the court across the street from her house. She would be aggressive and I did not mind the contact. Little did I know that her aggression on the court were the least of my worries.

I remember coming to see Paula one day and her mom said that she was up in her room and for me to go on up. I started making my way up the stairs and when I pushed open the door my life changed forever! There Paula stood with a plastic bag filled with crack. The room had a smell that was all too familiar because I had several family members using crack. Paula had attempted to mask the smell with air freshener, but that only made the scent stronger. I asked her what in the hell was she doing. She said that she was holding the drugs for her nephew. I asked her how could she do this to me and she said she did not know what I was talking about. I stormed back down the stairs and left.

Shortly after my discovery of Paula's drug use, she started saying that she did not know if having another baby was the right thing for her and that she was thinking about getting an abortion. She was stating that she no longer wanted our baby. I asked her how she could talk about aborting my baby when I was here helping her take care of her three kids. We fought and fought and finally it was too late for her to get an abortion. Thank you God for helping me protect my unborn child.

Paula and I began getting back on track with our lives. She said that she was committed to having the baby and that she would never use drugs again. We once again started enjoying being around each other and everything appeared to be normal. I was going to be a dad and I was very proud of that title. I would rush home after work to ask her how her medical appointments went; I could not go with her due to my work schedule. Paula said that the baby was healthy and strong. We had made the decision not to know the sex of the baby. It was crazy but I seemed to be the one gaining all the weight and I was the one that had all the sickness.

Paula was still worried about having another child with another baby's daddy and not being married. I told her that I would marry her and I promised her that when the baby was born we would be in our own home. I asked her to have faith and not to get so upset. We started to plan for our future and the kids were happy about me being in their lives.

I remember leaving Paula's house early in the morning of October 3, 1992 and telling her that I would come over later to see how she was feeling. At that point, she was due any day. I went home, to my grandmother's house, and lay across my bed. I was at home for a few hours when the phone rang. Paula was on the other line and she said, "I think it's time!" I was so excited! I asked her if she was sure. I told her "I'm on my way". I ran lights and I took back streets. That was the fastest I ever got to her house. We rushed to the hospital and the moment that was supposed to be the happiest moment in a father's life turned into the scariest moment in my life.

The nurse came into the room and asked how we were doing. I was the proud dad so I said we were good. She turned to Paula and said we have not seen you since your initial visit and normally that means one of two things: either you are in trouble with the law or you are using drugs. My face felt like stone and I could not move. The nurse said if you are using, the toxicology report will show it. I just remember looking at Paula and her saying that she was not using drugs. It was a strong silence in the room and at that moment I felt that I was back in the bedroom of her house and Paula was holding the bag of crack. My throat was dry and I could not catch my breath. My chest felt like someone had been sitting on it. I finally told her that if she was using I would do everything to take my baby. She denied using. The nurse came back a little later and the reports were positive. I just started crying and the nurse asked if we needed to talk to the social worker. I pulled myself together and said no. I started praying and making all kinds of deals with God. I remember saying that no matter how my child comes into this world, I will love that baby with all my heart and I would be there no matter what.

At 2:23 pm, Paula gave birth to a beautiful baby girl 7 pounds and 11 ounces. I was a DADDY! A FATHER! I had a baby girl with all her fingers and toes. I stood there and thanked God. We named her Desiree. On that day, I promised Desiree that I would be there for her and that I would never abandon her for any reason. I held her and promised her that I would protect her with my life.

We had a social worker come in during Paula's time in the hospital and she helped her to prepare for an outpatient rehab program. Paula was still trying to justify the drug use and she was claiming that she was not using that much. Paula promised that she would stay clean and that she wanted to keep our family together.

When we left the hospital I took Paula to our new home. Paula was so excited that we now had our own place. She looked like she was doing okay and that she was committed to our family. I was not buying into the new and improved Paula. At that point, I understood what I needed to do to protect my rights as a father. I knew that I could no longer trust her to tell me the truth.

I returned to work and told my supervisor that I needed to be able to take my child to all of her doctor's appointments and that this was nonnegotiable. I explained to her my situation and she was very sympathetic. I went to the first appointment and Paula was upset, saying that I did not trust her to take Desiree to the doctor. We made such a scene in the hospital that the social worker came out and took us into her office. I did not care what Paula thought about me coming to the doctor's office. I made a promise the day my child was born that I would always be there for her and I was going to keep it. Her life was a gift from God and I would protect it at any cost. The plan to be a father was at the top of my list. I was not going to be the missing dad like my father. I was not going to abandon my child.

I remember telling my mother that I was going to marry Paula, and she was livid. She told me that it was bad enough that I got with her and all those kids when I did not have any of my own, but now I wanted to marry her. She told me that I did not have to marry her to be a father to my child. I explained to my mother that Paula was using drugs and that Desiree was born a crack baby. I also told her that I have seen so many fathers lose their rights to be a father because they were not married to the mom. The courts did not respect father's rights and always seemed to side with mothers. I told my mom that I did not want to be that father who could only see his child when he and the mom were on good terms. I did not want to be the father who does not have the right to say how their child's life is shaped. My mom said that she understood and that she would support my decision. I remember thinking to myself, "Man, this is how women must feel when they are with a man for the sake of the child". I reflected back on my mom and all of the men that did not want to have anything to do with my brother and me. I made sure that I was a major part of all of the kids' lives. I continued to treat them like I was their dad.

I honestly thought I was no longer in love with Paula, but I could not leave the kids with her. I knew that she would not be right. Paula never did leave the drugs alone; she only pretended to be free of drugs. I continued with my plans of marriage. Paula was very reluctant to get married. She gave me some excuse saying being married would jinx us and we would only get divorced. I continued to give her all the reasons why we should be married and she finally said yes and we had a small ceremony.

Somewhere during that time I started feeling like this could work for us. I began to trust her and she appeared to be drug free. She was being a mommy and she was being a good wife, but I continued to go to all of Desiree's appointments. We were a family and things felt great.

The drug free Paula did not last for long. I remember coming downstairs and walking into our kitchen and witnessing a drug transaction between Paula and a neighborhood dope boy. He hurried up out the door and she started pretending that I did not see what had happened. I did not even argue with her. I smiled and thought to myself, "I will not be fooled again!" That day changed my perspective on life. I understood that I was not to be happy. My only quest was to protect the kids at any price.

Life with Paula was now a marriage of convenience. By this time Paula and I were really just going through the motions. I wanted out of the marriage and she wanted to be free too. I began cheating and Paula was doing her thing too. I finally asked her for a divorce and we started the procedures. I moved to the third floor and eventually started staying away from the house.

I wanted joint custody, but Paula would not bend. I told her that our child did not even want to be with her. Desiree was attending the preschool where I worked, and every time Paula would try to pick Desiree up from school she would scream and yell for me not to let mommy take her. It became so embarrassing for Paula. I eventually had to start bringing Desiree home and sitting with her before leaving.

I learned some valuable lessons as I went through the challenges of being married and being a father. My option to marry was a great opportunity to increase my chances of solidifying my role in my child's life. I am not advocating this for anyone because there should be better options for fathers to be a part of their child's life. Please review Appendix 1 for information on father's rights.

7

I am NOT My Father

I eventually moved out of the house. But unlike my father, I did not abandon my child. I would get up every morning at 4:30 am to catch three buses to pick Desiree up for school. Paula did not make the transition easy for me. I would have to knock on the door and hope she answered. When she did not answer, I had to go to the end of the street to a pay phone and have my mother call and keep calling to wake Paula up. Sometimes she would have Desiree ready and sometimes she would not. The days that she was not ready were the days that I would iron her clothes and try to make it to work on time. We would then run and catch the bus, even though Paula had a car.

The winter months were the worst, but we had a good time. I would put Desiree on my shoulders and we would make our way to the bus stop. We would always walk down this one street with a yard full of people figures. Desiree would talk to them and I would talk and pretend they were talking back. She really enjoyed me changing my voice. We had become such regulars on the bus the driver knew us. When we were a little late the bus driver knew we were coming and he would wait for us.

I continued to push for joint custody and one day Paula and I had a big argument and she told me to just take Desiree because she did not want to be there anyway. I packed up some things and we went to my mom's house. I told the woman I was seeing that I needed to be with my daughter and I did not want to confuse her with another woman. I took a break from that relationship and focused all my attention on my child. This was a great time, but Paula only allowed this for a few weeks.

I remember getting a call from my brother saying that Paula and her mother Nana came to the house and threatened to call the police if they did not give Desiree back to them. My mom had hidden Desiree in the closet and locked the family dog in the room to ensure no one would go inside. My mom and brother tried to stall them until I arrived, but it did not work. The fear of the police forced them to give Desiree to her mom. I just remember being on the bus and seeing Paula's mom's van crossing the intersection and Desiree kicking and screaming in the van's passenger seat.

I got home and my mom was crying telling me she tried to do everything to stop them, but she could not have the police come and start trouble. I rushed to Paula's house and at that moment all I could think about was killing her and getting my baby. This was the baby that I fought to bring into this world. This was the baby that I had sacrificed my life to keep. This was the baby that I vowed to protect for the rest of her life and with every breath in my body. My baby was now being taken from me.

Paula knew that I would come and that I would be mad as hell. She told me that she had called the police and that they were on their way. She said that I would never have her child around the bitch I was seeing. Paula was angry because someone had told her they had seen me out with my girlfriend. The crazy part of this was I never allowed Desiree to be around the young lady. I wanted Desiree to get comfortable with our new living situation before I introduced her to someone new in my life.

I understood that she was attempting to make me pay for not wanting to be with her anymore and that she was going to use our child to do it. I asked her if we could sit down and talk and see what we could come up with. We sat down and for the first time in a long time we were honest with each other. She told me how she felt alienated with regards to my new relationship. She told me that she felt that I had abandoned her. She said that she felt that at the moment she was putting her life together, I decided to leave. I told her that this was the first time that I felt I could leave. I told her that throughout her drug use I felt trapped and I felt like I was being punished for her decision to smoke crack and give up on the family.

That day I found out that Nana had put her up to getting Desiree back. She was the one pushing for me not to be a part of my child's life. I also found out that Paula allowed Nana to manipulate her into not allowing me to take the other kids with me for visits. She stated that I might treat them different. Paula made excuses why they could not come with me, and eventually I just accepted her decision. Through our conversation we verbally agreed on joint custody. The joint custody lasted for a few months and she was even allowing me to get the other kids every now and then. The feeling of having them all with me changed me in a major way. I was feeling like my babies were my world. Something happened and Paula's choices changed all of our lives forever.

It was May of 1996, I remember talking to Paula about me coming over and seeing the kids. Paula seemed to have been in a good mood and she was not tripping about me and my relationship. Paula was even allowing Desiree to spend time around my girlfriend without all the drama. I told her that I had something to do later on that day, but I would come and spend time with the kids when I dropped Desiree off the following day. She said okay and we joked with each other and we hung up. I was actually starting to think that we would be okay with the shared parenting and even with being friends. Paula was in school and she was enjoying her life and I was happy for her success.

Around 2pm that day, a co-worker came into the classroom and told us about how the police had a woman face down on the car and she seemed to be out of it. I checked it out and soon realized that the woman was Paula. Paula was being placed in the back of the police car and she still had on her pajama top. There had to be at least eight police cars surrounding her little red Mustang. Paula's hair was all over her head and she looked high. I slowly backed down the stairs and attempted to gather my thoughts. I was scared to go and ask what had happened. A million things rushed through my mind and I became nauseous. I rushed back to the preschool center and I told my co-worker that the lady in trouble was Paula and that I needed to make some calls to find out what was going on.

By the time I could get myself together to the make the calls, my pager was flooded with messages. Paula's mom had paged me, my mom was paging, and my brother was paging. Everyone wanted to let me know that Paula was arrested. I never told anyone that I had seen her being put in the police car. I remember thinking that I was so glad that my child was not outside. All I could do was wait and find out what she had done.

Later that day, Paula's mom called and told me that she had the other kids with her and that she was at the house getting them a few things. I went over to see if everyone was okay and that's when she said that Paula was being charged with armed robbery and kidnapping. Paula had attempted to rob an eyewear store and held the employees by gunpoint. I asked what the hell she was doing that for. She was unable to answer that question. She asked me if I could bring Desiree over to spend some time with her siblings. Even though it was my week to have her I told her that I would. That was a mistake.

Once I allowed Desiree to go there, Nana told me that Paula said that she was not to give Desiree back to me. I told Nana that it was not Paula's decision because the agreement that Paula and I made for shared custody could not happen with her being in jail. I told her that I would be willing to take all the kids home and continue to be their father until Paula was able to get out of this situation. Nana refused to hear me and she told me that I was not going to get my child back. I told her that I would see her in hell before I allowed her to take my child. I told her that I was the father and it was my responsibility to take care of my child and no one was going to stand in my way. That was the start of a war between us.

I contacted my lawyer and she told me that I could no longer serve Paula a dissolutionment while she was incarcerated. I now had to file for a full divorce and now I was seeking full custody of all the children.

I had to pay the lawyer another $5000.00 just for her to continue the case. I told her about Paula and Nana's plan to keep my child from me. She told me that I could take the police to her house and get Desiree, but Nana could stall them and it could get nasty. I asked her if I just took my child would it be kidnapping. She said that I could not kidnap my own child. What happened next was not fun, but it was necessary.

I called my friend, someone who I trusted with my life, to help me keep an eye on Nana while I was filing all the necessary paper work at the Justice Center. I told him what was going on and that I suspected Nana would try to send Desiree out of town with Paula's sister. My friend asked me what I wanted him to do if they attempted to send Desiree off with someone. I told him to do whatever was necessary to stop them. He knew exactly what that meant.

He and I were in constant contact during my trip to the Justice Center. He let me know that Nana had taken all of the kids to various places and that he was following. The last call came when he told me that the family was inside the legal aid office. I told him to sit tight because I was right next door. I met him out front and told him that I was going to go in and bring Desiree out and no matter what happens, He should get her to my mom.

I went inside and Nana was in the back talking to a lawyer. I hugged all the kids and Desiree was so happy to see me. She said, "Daddy, I missed you". She hugged me so tight. I remember thinking that we would never be separated again. Desiree was wearing a dirty white sailor outfit that was too tight and smelled of urine. I told the kids that I was taking her to the bathroom. I told them that I loved them very much. At that point, Darius said, "Daddy, can I go too?" The hardest thing for me to do was to tell him a lie. I told him I would come back and take him after I finish with Desiree. I knew that it would be kidnapping if I took him and I would go to jail.

I started walking out the door and I never looked back. I reached the door and I remember hearing Nana's voice telling me to stop. I just kept going. It seemed like my friend's car was a mile away from the building, even though it was just across the street. I reached the car and I gave Desiree to him. I grabbed his gun off the seat and turned towards Nana, I knew that she always carried a gun so I could not take any chances on her shooting me. I turned and pointed the gun at her and I told her that she had two options, she could turn around and walk back to the building or she could die out here in the street. Either way my child was going with me. Nana told me that this was not over and that she would get Desiree back and take care of me.

On my way home, I received a call from my brother. He was screaming through the phone asking me what in the hell I did. He said that Nana had called and said that she was sending the police to our house because I kidnapped Desiree. He was so scared and he wanted me to take her back to Nana. I told him that I could not kidnap my own child and that he needed to calm down. He told me he hoped I knew what in the hell I was doing because this could get everyone in trouble. He was terrified of the police finding out about his drug empire.

I then received a call from my girlfriend. She was screaming at me about Nana contacting her. She told me that Nana had threatened to hurt her and her child if they had anything else to do with me. She said that Nana told her of Paula's plans to kill her and that Paula had made keys to her building before she went to jail and that she had been following us around. I told her not to worry that I would make sure Nana never called her again.

I called Nana and I told her that if she ever threatened anyone else in my family again that I would kill her. She told me that she was recording our conversation and that she would use it against me. I was so angry that I told her I did not give a damn! I told her that she could record whatever she wanted. I then repeated myself: "If you threaten anyone else in my family again, I will kill you".

I asked Nana to take a moment and think about the fact that I knew where she was today. I went on to tell her of every stop she made during the day. There was complete silence on the phone. I told her that just like I knew where she was today, I could easily find her whenever I needed to. I told her that she was not the only one capable of reaching someone. I told her to ask Paula what I am capable of doing especially when it comes to my child. I then told her that if she contacted anyone else, we would see who reaches who first. Nana never bothered our family again. I later realized that I was completely out of my mind and fueled with rage. I never wanted to threaten anyone like that ever again. That day made me understand what a father would do to protect his child. I never had that protection from my father. I never knew what protection felt like from a man. I only knew that I would lay down my life to protect my child.

8

Becoming a Single Parent

Paula was sentenced to 4 to 15 years in a women's correctional institution. She was guaranteed to serve 4 years. Now the battle for custody began. Along with the divorce, the judge granted me full custody of Desiree. I had spent several thousand dollars attempting to get custody of all the children, but I did not have a legal leg to stand on. Of course Nana was fighting me every step of the way. When the judge gave me custody, he applauded my efforts to stand up and take responsibility of my child and the attempted efforts to gain custody of all the children. The judge said he wished he could give me all the children because he had no doubt that they would be better off with me.

The struggles to be a good father were hard enough, and now I was a single parent. I had full custody of a three year old girl. Lord, help me! This situation was going to be real interesting.

Life quickly changed for me and I had to make many sacrifices to ensure I was doing the right thing for my child. One of those sacrifices was my relationship with my girlfriend. Sometimes when people get involved they forget to talk about the "what ifs" in life. We never discussed what would happen if something happened to Paula. We never discussed what would happen if Desiree had to live with us fulltime. There was a strain on Desiree and my girlfriend to adjust to the new living situation. Desiree wanted her daddy's attention and my girlfriend though she was just being spoiled. The pressure from that situation forced me to reconsider my role as a father and as a future husband. I chose being a father first. I had to remove myself from the relationship because I needed to focus on Desiree. The abandonment of that relationship was difficult because we were making wedding plans. We had the rings and the hall and now here I was calling off the ceremony. I was the biggest monster and bad guy known to man.

Again, we make life altering choices as parents. I gave up a good relationship and a nice place to live to make sure my child was receiving what she needed from her dad. I moved back to my mom's basement and we started our new life. I had a fold-up bed and Desiree had a cot from the childcare center. We did not have much but we had each other.

My mom helped, but she did not have much of a childhood. She never learned to braid hair. I was glad that I knew how to do twist braids and plats. I would keep Desiree looking nice. I was organized and very meticulous about Desiree's clothing. I sorted her berets and hair balls by color and kept them in plastic containers. I matched her outfits with the hair accessories. It was so cool when people would compliment Desiree on her hair. People automatically thought that her mom was responsible for her hair. They would say, "Your mommy did a good job on your hair". She would say, "My daddy did my hair". That was an instant conversation for me to have with the lovely ladies.

I was very cautious with Desiree. I never let her out of my sight except when she was with grandma. I think sometimes I might have been too overbearing. I had such a fear that someone would try and take her from me that it might have created a dependency within me.

Times were a little rough for us both emotionally and financially. I was only working part-time as a preschool teacher and I did not have medical insurance. I really found out that the system was not designed for men who had custody of their children. Desiree was often sick and I had to pay out of pocket for her to go back and forth to the doctors.

I remember attempting to get help through various programs and was told that they were for woman and that I did not qualify. Then I started to receive Healthy Children Healthy Starts. Yet, the moment my income went over the required amount, I was cut off the program. My income was $11 over and they cut me off. Unbelievable! I could see why so many women feel like it was easier not to have a job and just collect the medical benefits for their children. I was caught between not working full-time to receive benefits and making too much to get any help from programs. The crazy thing was that once again I did not make enough to afford to take my baby to the doctors. I paid enough for them to bill me and we worked out the balances. Medical bills, food, and clothing are very expensive when you are only making a little more than minimum wage. But we survived.

I went back to my childhood roots and began putting Desiree's clothes in layaway. I would do the same thing my mom use to do for me. I put her outfits up every time I got paid and got them out within a month. When it was time to grocery shop, I started cutting coupons and making sure I knew when the stores had sales. I was truly becoming Mr. Mom. Taking care of my baby was the best job in the world. Even though it did not allow me to have much of a social life, it made me reflect back on the sacrifices my mom made for me.

Desiree and I developed a system for getting her clothes ready at night. She wanted to see what I was wearing and then she tried to match her outfits with mine. She always wanted to wear the same colors as me, so we had similar outfits. I would wear a vest and corduroys and so would she. Desiree was truly a daddy's girl. We would go to school looking like the proud twosome.

During her time in the childcare, Desiree was not very friendly. She only had one real friend and her name was Yssis. Yssis and Desiree seemed inseparable. They only wanted to play with each other and when one of them was not in school the other would cry and be upset. Yssis also was a product of a single parent home. Her mother Nicole was raising Yssis and living in her mother's attic.

Before long, Desiree and Yssis were attempting to hangout after school. When Nicole would pick Yssis up from school, Yssis would always ask if Desiree could come too. I had never let Desiree go anywhere without me or my mom, so that was totally out of the question. I would make all kinds of excuses for Desiree to remain right at the center with me

Then we started seeing Nicole and Yssis on the bus every morning. Nicole and I began to talk about the girls and how close they were with each other. We found out that their birthdays were three days apart. The more we would ride the bus the more we got to know each other. Eventually, I allowed Desiree to go on a play date with Yssis.

Desiree was so excited about going to Yssis' house and their family treated her like she was a member of their family. I remember Desiree coming home and talking about her auntie Debbie. I told her she did not have an auntie Debbie. Desiree said she did and that she was also Yssis's auntie. I later found out Auntie Debbie was Nicole's aunt. After being around Auntie Debbie and others, the challenge was now getting Desiree to want to stay home. I must admit it felt good to have a family structure for Desiree because she did not have much of a relationship with her siblings. The time she spent with Yssis helped to heal the absence of her sisters and brother.

Nicole was a great person to have around Desiree. She had such a genuine love for my baby and I did not have to force the relationship on Desiree. The more the girls started to hangout, the more Nicole and I hung out. I really started to enjoy our times together and it started to feel like we were a family. I would always call Nicole my cat.

The comfort level grew and grew and at one point Nicole asked me if I would go to a formal with her.I was so worried because I was a few years older than Nicole and she looked like a little kid. I was used to dating grown looking women and here was Nicole with her puffy coat, jeans, Timberland boots, and braids with a headband. I liked her, but I was not sure if I wanted to date her. I reluctantly said yes. I remember stressing out about what she was going to wear and if she was going to look old enough to be with me. I was acting as if Nicole was a teenager when, hell, she was only four years younger than me.

The night of the formal came and I picked Nicole up. Much to my surprise, she looked amazing. I was thinking to myself, "Man, what happened to the puffy coat girl with the torn jeans"? Nicole had taken her braids out and had a beautiful hairdo. She had on a beautiful black dress and man was it accentuating her curves. I did not know she had a body like that! Needless to say, she was not looking like a little kid. We went to the ball and Nicole and I danced the entire time. I watch her as she moved across the floor and her body moved like beautiful artwork.

Nicole and I became real close over the next few months. We would catch the bus to do Christmas shopping for the girls. Desiree and I started to spend more and more time with Nicole and Yssis. The more time we spent together, the more comfortable it became. Nicole was just what Desiree and I needed and the tension of Desiree's mom being gone started to lift. It started to feel like we were getting some structure to our lives and this was the happiest I had seen my child.

The personal time that Nicole was putting into Desiree was not the only blessings we received. My mom and my stepdad purchased a home and gave Desiree and me the finished third floor. We finally had a space for ourselves. I wasted no time buying bedroom sets and televisions for us and we were so proud of the new space. It was much better than living in the basement. Thanks be to God for continuing to look out for us. The third floor allowed me to spread out, and I had a kitchen sink and my own bathroom.

Living on the third floor allowed for company to come and visit. Nicole and Yssis wasted no time finding their way over to the new place. We spent many days cooking on a hotplate and watching the girls enjoy themselves. Eventually Nicole and I became romantically involved and those days hanging on the third floor turned into nights. We now were starting to become a blended family. The third floor did not last long.

During our time on the third floor, Nicole received news that she was chosen for section 8 housing. Nicole was so excited to be able to get her own place. I started helping her look for houses and eventually I helped her land a nice bungalow. The first day in her new house was exciting and Desiree and I was there to celebrate her blessing. I remember Yssis and Desiree coming out of the room and asking if we could spend the night. I looked and said no, we should go home. But Nicole started in with the girls and before long I was out-voted. The funny thing about spending the night was we never returned to the third floor. That day we became fully committed to being together. Once again, I found myself in a situation where I was involved with a blended family. I believed that I was better prepared to deal with this situation than I was in my previous marriage. I was a little nervous because I was still feeling out my emotions and long-term thoughts of what Nicole and I were doing with each other. The girls seem to be happy and Nicole was ecstatic. The role of becoming fully committed did not just start with Nicole, but also Yssis and Desiree. We were getting ready to embark on a journey into an area of total commitment to parenting two children together. Nicole and I only stayed in the new place for a year. We eventually moved out, purchased a home and got married. Now I was a husband and a step-father, AGAIN!

9

Understanding the Role of a Step-Father

Being a step-father is not an easy task. We often get into relationships with women who have children and we do not investigating the role we will play in their lives. We become so focused on the relationship between the two adults that we forget to ask about our role in the children's lives.

Being a step-father to Yssis was a little easier for me because I had been her teacher; discipline and understanding were already established from that perspective. Even though my role as her teacher helped, it did not prepare me for everything.

I remember the first time I had to discipline Yssis as her step-father. She and Desiree were getting into some mischief and I had to spank both their legs. I remember wondering if I was spanking her to hard or if I was being harder on Desiree than Yssis. These were thoughts that often bounced through my mind over the years. I am sure that many men who have blended families think about the issue of discipline. Are we being harder or more lenient on our biological child versus our step-child? Over the years I just attempted to do more talking and less physical punishments. I think the results worked out well.

As step-fathers we must still establish primary rules in the house that every child must follow. We must decide on punishments if those rules are broken. One of the things that I would do with Yssis and Desiree was to allow them to help establish the punishments for their actions. This was a major help because it allowed them to see team unity in the family. Another area in which we operated as a family was the famous family meeting. If any of the girls believed that Nicole and I were being unfair about a punishment they could call a family meeting and argue their case.

Nicole and I would meet and revisit the situation and give them a final decision. The girls really enjoyed this because sometimes they would present very valid reasoning and the case was overturned.

Life as a step-father may require you to deal with the biological father at some point. Yssis' dad was in her life on limited bases and he and I knew each other prior to me meeting Nicole. I never knew he was Yssis dad, but once I found out, I was cool.

My philosophy in handling Yssis' dad was that there is room in her life to have two dads. I would cook dinner and invite him and his girlfriend over. We would sit back and talk and laugh about things we had in common. These days seem to be great for Yssis because she did not have to feel pressure if she wanted to spend time with her biological dad.

We would also invite Yssis' cousins, aunt, and grandmother over so that they too could be a part of our life. The cousins called me Uncle Mel and I thought we were all going to have a great relationship. Yssis' aunt, who was Nicole's best friend, would come and get the girls to hang out with her kids. Then things changed.

One day Nicole received a letter in the mail from the Department of Human Services stating that Yssis' dad would have to start paying the state funds for the time Nicole and Yssis had been on public assistance. The letter also stated that he would have to pay child support to Nicole.

When he found out that he had to pay the state and give Nicole over $12,000 in back support, he was heated. I attempted to allow Nicole to handle the situation in an effort to keep the peace. Nicole explained to him that this had nothing to do with her reporting him, but the system just caught up with him.

I remember him telling her that he should not have to have the white man in his business because he takes care of his child. That was kind of funny considering he would only purchase her things on her birthday and on Christmas. Sometimes he would come at the end of summer with clothes from the clearance rack that would be too small by next summer.

He told Nicole that she had better write a letter to the state releasing him from any back support and any other obligations, because he takes care of his child. Once again, Nicole attempted to explain to him that we take care of Yssis and that it was my income that pays for all of her social activities and various programs. He did not like the sound of that message. The final conversation with him ended when he called Nicole some very unnecessary names and threatened her. Now it was time for me to handle the situation.

I took the phone from her and explained to him that I did not disrespect my wife, and I would not allow him to be disrespectful. I guess with all the energy floating in the air he decided to use the same language with me. He told me to stay the fuck out of their business and graciously reminded me that I was not Yssis' dad. He told me everything that he would do to me. Wow, this coming from the man I opened my home to with open arms. This coming from the man I attempted to keep in his child's life, because I knew what it was like for a child to feel abandoned by their dad. I was appalled by his actions. After a few minutes of his antics, I told him that he was no longer welcome in my home and that if he continued to make threats I would take action the next time I see him. Let's just say he continued to make threats and I did see him.

Shortly after me seeing him, Yssis received a letter in the mail along with a piggy bank and some photos of him. The letter stated that daddy would not be coming around for a while and that he loved her. When he stopped coming around, so did his family. That was painful because I was a part of the kids' lives and I thought Nicole and the aunt's relationship was much more solid.

I learned a valuable lesson in dealing with my role as a step-father. As a step-father we must establish rules and guidelines for respectable communication. We must be mindful of what is most important: the child. We must understand that there might be some unresolved feelings or some insecurity with the biological father regarding our roles in their child's life. Regardless of the situation, understand that we are responsible for the safety and welfare of our family. In the end, our obligation is to provide the best foundation for our household. If the biological father cannot respect the foundation and principles of our home, then we must make sure that all legal precautions are in place to protect our family.

Through all the struggles of blending our family and facing the challenges of being a step-father, Nicole and I gave birth to a beautiful baby girl named Taylor. Taylor is a kid that closed the family circle. She is the kid that makes all the family members understand the importance of family. I truly believe God sent her to keep all of us together. She has the gift to gab like her father and a big warm heart like her mother. All of my girls are unique and special to me and I see them as blessings from God.

10

Letters to My Daughters

We sometimes forget to tell our children what they mean to us. We sometimes get caught up in the day to day excitement of life that we do not see each other as much as we would like. We look up and the kids are grown and exploring their own lives. I asked my children would it be okay to share my letters to them with the world. So I wanted to pause here and dedicate a chapter of the book to letters for each of my girls. We have gone through so many things and each one of them has had a profound impact on how I see life.

Dear Desiree,

When I think about my life, I realize nothing in it was important until you were born. The moment I knew I was going to be a dad was the beginning of my life. I think back on all the challenges we had to face and I smile because I know that you were the one that saved my life. You gave me a purpose and a desire to be the best that I could be.

Desi, sometimes I find myself looking at you when you walk into the room, and thinking, "Here is my young lady". It's hard to believe that you are all grown up and in college. It seems like yesterday that you were the little girl that would hold on to her daddy's arm and make sure no one was going to get close. You were the baby who would sit down at night while daddy did your hair.

I think back on the days we had to sleep in the basement and how we had to get creative with the bathroom situation you know what I'm talking about! We made it work and we had plenty of good laughs. Do you remember the time when your grandma tried to do your hair and you called me crying? I had to come home and redo your hair. That was funny. Remember how you could never attend sleepovers without calling me wanting to come home? Hell, you were calling me all the way up until your after prom. I thought I was going to have to drive and pick you up from your own senior event. You are still that little girl at heart.

Desi I know that I have made some mistakes along the way, but everything that I have ever done was to provide a better life for you. I wouldn't trade any of the ups and downs we have had to endure if it meant that I couldn't have you as my child.

I know that you are legally an adult, but you will always be daddy's baby. You and I fight over some of the choices you make in your life, but I know you still have the foundation that has been built inside of you. I know that when all the smoke clears, you will make the decisions that will keep you focused.

Desi, I am so proud to be your dad and I thank you for keeping me on my toes. You are truly your own person, and out of all my children, I think you have the biggest heart. I think that you are one of the most compassionate people I have ever met. Please remember to follow your path and never stop believing in yourself. I know that I won't!

Love Daddy!

Dear Yssis,

Yssis, you are the daughter that God blessed me with to ensure that your sisters will stay focused. I never imagined when you walked into my classroom that I would one day become your dad. You have shown me that nurture as well as nature can make us family. I may not be your biological father, but I am your dad.

Yssis, you are my child that is most like me in terms of being responsible. You are the one that attempts to make everything right for everyone. You are the child that takes care of business first! I look at you and I see me. I am so proud of the young lady you have become.

I love when you just want to hang out with me, even if it's only you and I. I often laugh when I think about how much you look forward to seeking me out when you needed things to be handled. You make me feel like the proud father because you truly believe that there is nothing I can't handle.

I never told you, but I started to cry when I thought about you going away to Ohio State University. I told your mom that I didn't want my baby to leave me. I didn't want to come home to a house where you are not there to greet me. I love when you come home and say, "Hey peeps". I love when you whine about wanting to do things as a family. I will miss you stealing my remote when you think I'm a sleep.

I know OSU is only two hours away, but it will seem like a lifetime away because I can't see you every night. I know that you will be responsible and that you will attempt to do your best to succeed in life.

Yssis, always remember that no matter what happens in life, your dad is so proud of you. I could not have asked for a better child to call my daughter. I love you. Dad!

Dear Taylor,

Ms. Taylor, the true meaning of DADDY'S little girl. Your mom always says that the day you came home from the hospital was the day you became a daddy's girl. I remember taking you down stairs that night and singing to you. You just had a glow in your eyes and from that point forward we have been partners.

Tay, you were a handful when you were learning to walk. Your mom and I would always have to tell you to stay off the steps and out of the kitchen, not to mention trying to stop you from eating paper towels. One of the funniest memories was when you wanted to nurse on me. I couldn't laydown in bed without a shirt because you always latched on to my chest.

Looking at you now, I believe you are the kid that will be the creative super star of the family. Your imagination and sense of humor is truly a blessing from God. I marvel over the fact that you can create just about anything. Buying you a hot glue gun was probably the best investment we ever made.

I often tell people that I think your sisters were the experiments so that I could get fatherhood right for you. I love the relationship that we share. I think I am a lot calmer as a parent when it comes to you. Your sisters say that you can get anything you want, but we know that's not true.

I love our daddy-daughter dates together. I love when we just hang out at restaurants or when we go shopping. You truly have my fashion sense. The greatest part of hanging out is that we truly enjoy each other's company. We can be gone for hours and continue laughing and joking the entire time.

Tay, you make me so proud to be a father and I can't wait to see what your future will bring us. Daddy loves you. Keep on having your own identity, that's what makes you stand out from everyone.

Love Daddy

To My Girls,

Each of you represents a beacon of light. This light will guide you towards your life's journey. The path towards success may get rough at times, but always remember that faith and prayer will never fail you. Each of you is a product of God, so please understand that if you walk in his purpose, there is nothing you can't accomplish.

My beautiful young ladies you have blessed me with the opportunity to help mold your lives and I can only hope that I have not failed you in my attempt. It is your strength that strengthens me in all that I do. As a father, I stand proud to affirm your goals and aspirations.

I look forward to seeing what the future holds for each one of you. I see your childhood personalities transforming into your personal accomplishments and I can only sit back and smile. God bless you all and know that daddy loves you!

11

Forgiving and Healing

Forgiving and healing is an area that many people never achieve when someone has hurt them. We tend to go through life with a chip on our shoulders, wanting everyone to pay a price for all the pain someone else caused.

Throughout my life I never realized how much anger I had against my father and any other man that hurt my mom. I never forgave, so, therefore, I never healed. It was not until a friend told me that in order to heal yourself you must forgive those who have hurt you. I remember thinking that I knew that old saying. Hey, I go to church and I know what the bible says about forgiveness. But, sometimes scars are so deep that we pretend they are no longer an issue. We say all the right Christian things, but we still hold on to the pain until it manifest in other areas of our lives.

Through self-evaluation I began to see that I spoke all the right words, but deep down I was angry and the scars were present in many of my personal and professional relationships.

The first opportunity I had to realize just how much I needed healing was when my sister got married. I had an opportunity to sit and talk with both my sisters about the role my dad played in their lives and their children's lives. The man they described was unfamiliar to me. This man was warm, gentle, and extremely loved by his family. He had given them all the love that I thirsted for my entire life. I really did not know how to handle that information. Once again, I came to the realization that I was hurt and I had yet to heal the wounds from my abandonment.

I met my father a few days prior to my sister's wedding and that was the first face-to-face conversation he and I had ever experienced. I could see the resemblance that my sister often spoke of. I was now standing face-to-face with the man that left my mom and me. I was now standing here with the man that never taught me to ride a bike or drive a car. This was the man whom I cried for at night to come and rescue us from the violence my mother had to endure. How could I even begin to talk of forgiveness? How could I heal from all that was missing in my life?

I had to reflect back on all that I had learned in scripture. I had to dig deep within and look for all that I proclaimed myself to be in Christ. The first passage that came to mind during my encounter was Colossians 3:21: **"Fathers, do not embitter your children, or they will become discouraged".** I was embittered and discourage because of his absence. I did not know what to say to the man that I vowed never to speak to in life.

He looked at me and started talking about all my accomplishments. He told me that he had been keeping track of me through relatives. He said he thought it was best not to upset my life. Then he wanted to tell me about the combative relationship he and my mother had. I stopped him at that point and simply told him, "Regardless of the relationship you had with her, at what point couldn't you have reached out to me?" "At what point could you have allowed me to make the decision to have you in or out of my life?" I told him the sad part of this conversation was that my mother never slandered him. I told him that I just wished he would have attempted to reach out and connect to his only son. That moment was the start of me forgiving and healing.

Shortly after meeting with my father, my mom and I attended my sister's wedding. My mom had an opportunity to speak to my father. The conversation was just an exchange of pleasantries. I could see it was an awkward moment for both of them. I never knew that my sister's wedding would be the last opportunity for me to have a conversation with my father. We had made plans to talk again, but he passed away shortly after the wedding.

I now had to think about all the things we never got to say to each other. How do I now attend a funeral of a man I never really knew? My sisters needed the support of their big brother, and so I put aside the many unanswered questions. I even cut his hair while he was being prepped for service. During that moment, I leaned over and said I forgive you for not being there. I whispered, as my eyes filled with tears, "I love you."

It is moments like death that you find yourself thinking that you never hated the person, but was so hurt because of their absence you blocked the love. Burying my dad unveiled the fact that I only wanted to love him and because he was not there, I was angry, hurt, and mad at the world. This encounter made me think of ways to help others learn how to heal and forgive those that have hurt them through abandonment, abuse, or any other type of hurt. Please see Appendix 2 for some techniques I use to forgive and heal.

Appendix 1

Men, here are some options afforded to you as a parent. The rights may vary from state to state, but the basic premise is the same in each state. Please check the laws in your state. Women, by making men responsible under your state's laws it ensures they will be legally obligated to take care of their responsibilities.

> ➤ Fathers need to establish paternity. In family law across the United States, if a married couple has a baby, the legal presumption is that the husband in that family is the father of the baby. But when a child is born outside of marriage, there is no legal presumption of paternity. Without establishing paternity, an unwed father has no legal standing as it relates to visitation, shared custody or the ability to make decisions about the welfare of the child. The simplest way to establish paternity is to make sure that the unwed father's name is on the baby's birth certificate. Being with the mother at the hospital when the baby is born and helping her fill out the birth certificate forms is the

least complicated way. If that is not possible, an unwed father can complete a Voluntary Acknowledgment of Paternity form in his state. If the mother contests the father's paternity, he can contact a government agency like the Child Support Enforcement Division in his state or he can petition a court to establish his paternity. The unwed father will need to take a paternity test (for which a court may order the mother's cooperation) to establish his parental status.

➢ Fathers need to Gain custody rights. Once an unwed father establishes paternity, he needs to work to determine his custody status. A man who is legally designated as the father has the same custody rights as a married father. If the unwed father and mother are raising the child together in the same home, custody is not an issue. But if at any time they separate, or if they are not intending to raise the child together, the father will need to petition a court to establish custody rights.

Fathers are generally at a disadvantage in a custody process because government agencies and family court judges usually start with the presumption that a child should be with his or her mother unless her custody would be detrimental to the child. So fathers who want custody of the child need to retain a family law attorney and start the legal process to establish custody.

In most cases, unless the mother is clearly unfit, the father will want to petition for joint or shared custody or he may want to allow the mother to have full custody with him only having visitation rights. If the mother is unfit to have custody of the child, he will want to petition for full legal custody. Before a court determines legal custody for the child, the parents should get together and establish a parenting plan that defines roles and responsibilities. When this can be done in a friendly way between the parents, the courts likely to approve the plan they create.

> Fathers need to pay child support. Men who are fathers, regardless of their custody status, have financial responsibility for a child. The only

way to avoid child support is for a father to have his paternity rights terminated which forever severs him from his child. If a father and mother are raising the child together, financial support happens informally. But if the parents separate, child support will become a formal legal obligation. Child support is determined based on a number of factors including the parents' individual income levels and obligations, availability of other financial support, and the needs of the children. Each case is individual and the amounts of child support will be individually determined. But once child support is set by the courts, it becomes a primary financial obligation which can be enforced by government agencies. And whether or not the father has cooperation from the mother on things like visitation, child support obligations remain. Unwed fathers have rights and responsibilities like any other fathers do. But given the lack of a legal marriage between the parents, establishing those rights and enforcing those obligations become infinitely more complicated. Men, who find themselves as unwed parents, whether intentionally or not, need to take appropriate steps to ensure their parental rights and to meet their parental obligations. It is not a matter to be taken lightly when the life of a child is stake.

The tips that I have given should help men avoid taking the extreme measures that I took. In most cases, the courts still rule in favor of the mother, but our rights are being advocated more and more. Just do not give up on your child.

Appendix 2

Forgiveness and Healing Techniques

➤ Write a letter to the person that hurt you. This technique really helped me to get out all the hidden feelings that I had for my dad. I did this after he had passed. It's not so much about sending the letter than it is confronting your own pain. Talk about everything that you have been feeling and at the end of the letter simply say, "I forgive you!" Forgiving the person releases you from your own personal hell.

➤ Make a chart of all the things that were missing in your life either because you were abandoned or because you just had a rough childhood. The list should reflect all the things you liked about your childhood on one side and all the things you didn't on the other side. This list can become your road map to being a better parent to your child.

There is no full proof plan to parenting, but we have to start somewhere. At least, if we had some concept of how we want to treat our children then we might not make some of the mistakes that were made with us.

➢ Talk to your children. Children understand that life is challenging and parents make mistake. The biggest mistake we make is not communicating with our children. We take for granted that the children don't understand life's situations.

Reader's Guide to *Break the Cycle of Abandonment*

DISCUSSION QUESTIONS

Discuss Melvin's quest to have a father in his life. Do you think that not having a father helped or hindered his ability to be successful in his life? Do you think that knowledge or lack of knowledge about your family background shaped your personal self-image? Do you think that Melvin was destined to become who he is now regardless of whether the father was in the home?

Melvin and Michael both struggled to find their identities and each chose their own path. Do you think that their struggles against each other were partially their mother's fault because she appeared to have given up on Michael? Do you think had their mother stood firm with Michael that he would not have fallen victim to the streets?

How do you feel about Arlene pointing a gun at Melvin, and the use of a belt when he was caught stealing?

Melvin's love for and desire to protect his brother often made him a target for gang violence. Do you believe that you could have accepted the trauma that Michael's life placed on his family? Could you denounce your sibling?

Melvin's decision to marry Paula was clearly out of a need to protect his child. Do you think if he understood the legal path to take he would still have married her?

Do you think that Melvin ever stopped loving Paula, or did he just become so upset with the lies that he simply gave up?

Do you think that Melvin should have allowed Desiree to stay with her siblings? Do you think he went too far in his desire to protect his interest as a father? Could you have done what he did?

Melvin attempted to allow Yssis' dad in her life; do you think there were other measures that he could have taken to keep their relationship strong? Was he wrong to interfere in the conversation between Nicole and Yssis' dad?

Melvin often spoke of God and keeping his faith; do you think that his faith was the reason he forgave his dad?

forgiveness and healing is a chapter in the book. Do you think that people ever really heal from so much emotional trauma?

Do you think that you would have sacrificed as much as Melvin did to protect his rights to his child?

Made in the USA
Monee, IL
09 February 2024

53223499R00069